The

OVERLY HONEST

BABY BOOK

ISBN 978-1-58005-639-7

Library of Congress Cataloging-in-Publication Data is available.

Published by Seal Press, an imprint of Perseus Books, LLC,
a subsidiary of Hachette Book Group, Inc.
1700 Fourth Street
Berkeley, California
Sealpress.com

Cover design by Faceout Studio
Interior design by Megan Jones Design
Illustrations by Jill Howarth

Printed in the United States of America

The OVERLY HONEST

BABY BOOK

Uncensored
Memories from Baby's First Year

DAWN DAIS

Illustrations by Jill Howarth

SEAL PRESS

Contents

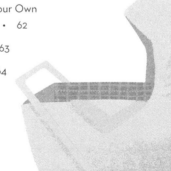

Introduction

Dear _____,

Welcome to the world, little one! We're all so excited you're here! You have brought with you an abundance of love and light, laughter and joy.

But, if we're being honest, you've also brought your fair share of tears and sleep deprivation, poop and spit-up.

While other baby books tend to focus on all the wonderful parts of babyhood, this book is different. This book is honest. And, spoiler alert: there are a lot of parts of babyhood that aren't so wonderful.

The Overly Honest Baby Book is here to give you a frank look at the first year of your life. So, instead of focusing on only smiles and adorableness, we're also going to shine a light on some of your less flattering achievements. For instance, the first time you spit up into your parent's open mouth is an important milestone that gets overlooked in traditional baby books. But not this one.

And no kid should ever have to go through life wondering when they first managed to poop into their own ear. This book you hold in your very hands will provide you the answer to that age-old question. You're welcome.

But this book isn't just focused on your milestones; it'll also provide a glimpse into how your first year on this earth affected your parents. (These details might finally explain why they always look so frazzled.)

Not every baby book records the first time Mommy accidentally let your stroller roll into traffic, or the last time she bathed herself two days in a row. But *The Overly Honest Baby Book* finally gives your parents a place to make note of these first-year highlights.

Also, we think it's important for you to know exactly how many f-bombs Mommy let fly during your delivery. Because you deserve the truth.

As you skim through this little book, try to remember that it was written by people who love you more than anything in the whole world. This time capsule, with all its honesty and horror stories, should be a constant reminder of that fact. Because only people who really, really love you would put up with all the crap you threw their way during your first year—and yes, you literally threw crap.

So read on to get an overly honest look at your first year. It's full of laughter, poop, cursing, and crying. And that's just your birth story.

Kisses!

_____

Your Loving Parents

Your Parents

THE BIRDS, THE BEES, AND MODERN MEDICINE

Families come in all shapes and sizes. Some even need a little help from a turkey baster. Here is how you came to be:

☐ Mom: _____ Dad: _____

Fertility doctor: _____

☐ Mom: _____ Mom: _____

Sperm bank: _____ Donor #: _____

Adoption agency: _____

☐ Dad: _____ Dad: _____

Surrogate name: _____

Adoption agency: _____

☐ Mom: _____

Asshole Who Was Not Ready for a Commitment: _____

Possible biological father #1: _____

Possible biological father #2: _____

Sperm bank: _____ Donor #: _____

Adoption agency: _____

Other: _____

Your Conception

SO MUCH MAGIC
(AND MAYBE ALSO A LITTLE INTOXICATION)

Date (*approximate*): _____

How much booze was involved: _____

The form of failed contraception that brought you into the world:

_____

The number of fertility doctors/nurses involved in this most natural of human processes: _____

The number of turkey basters involved in this most natural of human processes: _____

The various curse words Mommy uttered when she saw the positive symbol on her pregnancy test:

_____ / _____ / _____ / _____

The number of additional pregnancy tests
Mommy took just to be sure: _____

Joys of Pregnancy

SUCH A BEAUTIFUL TIME!
(IF YOU DON'T COUNT THE VOMITING, EXHAUSTION, AND IRRITABILITY)

The foods Mommy craved: _____

_____

The foods that made Mommy want to vomit: _____

_____

The smells that made Mommy want to vomit: _____

_____

BY THE NUMBERS

The number of hours a day Mommy had "morning" sickness: _____

The most times Mommy peed in one day while pregnant: _____

How much Mommy missed booze while pregnant: _____

The number of foods that didn't give Mommy heartburn: _____

The number of pounds Mommy gained: _____

WEEK BY WEEK

The week Mommy officially embraced maternity pants: _____

The week Mommy signed up for prenatal yoga: _____

The week Mommy stopped going to prenatal yoga: _____

The week Mommy's belly button popped out: _____

The week Mommy officially started to waddle: _____

The week Mommy officially could no longer tie her shoes: _____

The week Mommy was officially over being pregnant: _____

A Brief Pregnancy Diary

MIRACLES AREN'T EASY

First trimester (*the ways in which growing a placenta has kicked Mommy's ass*):

_____
_____
_____
_____
_____

Second trimester (*the details of some very weird dreams Mommy's been having*):

_____
_____
_____
_____
_____

Third trimester (*the ways in which the watermelon inside Mommy is attacking her organs*): _____

_____
_____
_____
_____

The last month (*the things Mommy hates because she's so done being pregnant*):

_____
_____
_____
_____

Pregnancy Photos

THE ALARMING THINGS HAPPENING TO MOMMY

First trimester
(Mommy thinks she looks fat)

Second trimester
(Mommy is developing
a love of chocolate ice cream
and a hatred of scales)

Your most alien-looking ultrasound

An ultrasound of your feet
kicking Mommy's bladder
(your favorite way to pass the time)

Your Baby Shower(s)

A RITUAL IN WHICH PEOPLE EXCHANGE ONESIES FOR MIMOSAS

The number of showers we needed to accumulate stuff for a person anticipated to weigh less than 10 pounds: _____

Who hosted your shower(s): _____

How much time they spent on Pinterest researching adorable baby shower ideas: _____

Some of the annoyingly adorable games guests were made to play:

_____

_____

The name of the partygoer who became surprisingly competitive during these games, apparently ready to fight to the death for the scented candle being given out as a prize: _____

The number of times Mommy/Daddy exclaimed, "Oh my goodness, so cute!" or "Adorable!" when opening gifts we'd requested/registered for:

_____

The name of the single friend who came to the afternoon shower clearly hungover: _____

How much money we made when we returned half the crap we received at your shower(s): _____

BY THE NUMBERS

Some of the baby-themed appetizers offered at your shower(s):

_____

The number of relatives who attended: _____

The number of friends at the shower who already had kids and were suspiciously ecstatic that another friend was pummeling toward parenthood: _____

The number of friends at the shower who didn't have kids, didn't participate in the games, and just drank mimosas for the duration: _____

OPTIONAL: The number of drinks Daddy had at his "Diapers and Beer" shower: _____

ONESIES BREAKDOWN

- The number of onesies we received: _____
- The cutest onesie (*describe*): _____
- The most sarcastic onesie (*describe*): _____
- The best "My First Holiday" onesie (*describe*): _____

Preparing for You

IT'S CUTE THAT WE ACTUALLY THOUGHT WE WERE PREPARED

The number of dollars (in thousands) spent on baby whatnots that you used for approximately 4 minutes after you arrived: _____

The number of trips to Babies"R"Us before you were born: _____

The number of Amazon deliveries after you were born: _____

The number of toys purchased for you: _____

The single toy we should have purchased: Tupperware.

The number of items purchased for you to sleep on or in: _____

The places where you actually slept: on Mommy/Daddy.

The theme of your nursery: _____

Where you ended up sleeping: on Mommy/Daddy.

The room in the house used for your nursery:

- ☐ Spare room
- ☐ Daddy's Man Cave
- ☐ Mommy's Craft Room
- ☐ Closet*
- ☐ Your Parents' Room*

* Spoiler Alert: Yours was an unplanned pregnancy.

Baby-Proofing Items Purchased to Prepare for Your Arrival

AS IF YOU WOULD BE RUNNING AROUND 5 MINUTES AFTER BIRTH

IF YOU WERE THE FIRST BABY

- [ ] 356 child locks
- [ ] 4 BABY ON BOARD signs (1 for each side of the car)
- [ ] 5 baby gates
- [ ] 234 outlet covers
- [ ] Padding for every sharp edge/ corner in the house
- [ ] Barricade around the fireplace
- [ ] Toilet seat locks
- [ ] TV straps to attach TV to the wall
- [ ] Furniture straps to attach furniture to the wall

- [ ] 42 cord covers
- [ ] Window locks
- [ ] Door locks
- [ ] 10 hooks for securing the cords from the window blinds/shades so they didn't strangle you
- [ ] KIDS AT PLAY sign for the front yard (*though you wouldn't actually play there for a number of years*)

IF YOU WERE THE SECOND (OR THIRD, OR FOURTH, ETC.) BABY

- [ ] Boxes grabbed from the garage to keep you from climbing up the stairs

The Year You Were Born

ALSO KNOWN AS THE YEAR YOUR PARENTS STOPPED BEING FUN

FUN FACTS

Your birth year: _____

The U.S. president at the time:

_____

The most annoying celebrity:

_____

The popular TV shows that your parents never again had time to watch:

_____

The most unfortunate hairstyle trend:

_____

The piece of clothing Mommy will regret having owned:

_____

The ways our generation is ruining everything for your generation:

_____

_____

_____

HOW MUCH STUFF COST WHEN YOU WERE BORN

Gallon of milk: $ _____

Vodka: $ _____

Gallon of ice cream: $ _____

Takeout from the deli: $ _____

Dozen eggs: _____

Box of tampons: $ _____

Box of cereal: $ _____

Twelve-pack of soda: $ _____

(This is pretty much all Mommy shopped for
before she got pregnant with you.)

Six-pack of wine: $ _____

Pack of condoms (wasted money): $ _____

Haircut (back when Mommy actually looked presentable): $ _____

Movie ticket (to see a show with cursing!): $ _____

Dinner out at a restaurant (aka pretty much every dinner): $ _____

(This is pretty much how Mommy spent her weekends
before she got pregnant with you.)

Package of diapers: $ _____

Headache medicine: $ _____

(This is pretty much all Mommy
shops for since having you.)

Your Team

THE PEOPLE WHO WILL
BAIL YOU OUT IN 18 YEARS

Grandma: _____

Grandpa: _____

Grandma: _____

Grandpa: _____

Grandma: _____

Grandpa: _____

Grandma: _____

Grandpa: _____

Aunts (some blood-related, most just women Mommy drinks wine with):

_____

_____

Uncles (aka guys who will think it's funny to let you drink their beer at
6 months old):

_____

_____

Neighbors/friends/cousins/babysitters/Amazon delivery person:

_____

_____

HERE'S WHAT SOME IMPORTANT PEOPLE LOOKED LIKE BEFORE THEY GOT OLD.

(name/relationship)

(name/relationship)

(name/relationship)

(name/relationship)

(name/relationship)

Your Birth

THERE WAS NO F'N STORK

THE PLAN

Mommy's birth plan: _____
_____
_____
_____
_____

Ways in which Mommy's birth plan was actually followed:
_____

All the things that were going wrong with your delivery though we were repeatedly told everything was fine: _____
_____

THE PLAYERS

The doctor's name: _____

The midwife's name: _____

The doula's name: _____

The nurses' names: _____
_____

The name of the nurse your parents wanted to take home with them because he/she was clearly more qualified to raise a child:
_____

The names of the 15 other random people who stopped by during or after your birth for no apparent reason: _____
_____
_____
_____

THE EPITHETS

How Mommy would describe childbirth (*check all that apply*):

☐ "Like I pooped out a baby"

☐ "Like someone ran over my body with a dump truck then pulled a melon out of my vagina"

☐ "A pain I will never, ever, ever forget"

☐ "Holy shit"

☐ "The most beautiful experience of my life"
(*in reference to the epidural kicking in*)

☐ The words "cut" and "tear" were used in reference to my lady parts—that's all you really need to know

☐ Other: _____
_____
_____
_____

THE NUMBERS

The number of f-bombs dropped: _____

How long Mommy was in labor (in days): _____

How far apart the contractions were when Mommy started demanding "ALL THE DRUGS!": _____

How many miserable hours Mommy tried to get you to come out before having a C-section: _____

The number of people Mommy kicked in the face: _____

The number of times Mommy changed her mind about this whole thing: _____

How private Mommy was before giving birth:

[1] ---- [2] ---- [3] ---- [4] ---- [5] ---- [6] ---- [7] ---- [8] ---- [9] ---- [10]

SHOWERED WITH   ANSWERED THE
CLOTHES ON   DOOR TOPLESS

How many complete strangers stared at Mommy's lady bits as she was giving birth:

[1] ---- [2] ---- [3] ---- [4] ---- [5] ---- [6] ---- [7] ---- [8] ---- [9] ---- [10]

JUST THE DOCTOR   THE ENTIRE
                                                              HOSPITAL STAFF

What Mommy looked like before she got pregnant

What Mommy looked like while trying to get you out of her body (this will explain a lot about Mommy)

Your Birth Story

HOW IT ALL WENT DOWN

_____
_____
_____
_____
_____
_____
_____
_____
_____
_____
_____
_____
_____
_____
_____
_____
_____
_____
_____
_____
_____
_____

Your Stats

SURELY THIS IS INTERESTING TO SOMEONE

Date of birth: _____

Time of birth: _____

Sex (*check all that apply*): ☐ Female   ☐ Male

Weight: _____

Length: _____

Circumference of your head (*do the math on that one and skip the attitude you're planning for your teen years*): _____

Eye color: _____

Hair color (*if applicable*): _____

    ☐ You have no hair

    ☐ You have a little hair

    ☐ You look like a dust bunny with eyes

What you looked like when you popped out:

    ☐ A raisin

    ☐ A 90-year-old man

    ☐ An alien who'd been swimming for 9 months

Your Name

IT SEEMED LIKE A GOOD IDEA AT THE TIME

Your name: _____

Reasons we liked this name: _____
_____

How much we'd been drinking when we chose it: _____

Close calls (horrible names we almost picked): _____
_____

How your parents chose your name:

- ☐ Out of a hat

- ☐ It was the least offensive name on our list of options

- ☐ Singing "Eeny, Meeny, Miney, Moe" while flipping through a baby name book

- ☐ We argued for months and finally gave up and named you after a character on a late-night cable show

- ☐ You were named after an extremely attractive actor/actress despite the fact that there's a good chance only someone extremely attractive can pull off that name (*sorry; and good luck with that*)

- ☐ We named you after a nice custodian in the hospital

- ☐ We got it from an Internet search of "cool names that won't get my kid's ass kicked"

Ways in which you'll be getting your ass kicked because of this name:
_____
_____
_____
_____

Your Horrible First Photos

WE SWEAR WE THOUGHT YOU WERE CUTE— THAT'S WHY WE TOOK SO MANY

Proof that we should have hired
a professional photographer
(with access to editing software)

Something seems to have
gone terribly wrong here

No one in the family is flattered
when told you look just like them

The photo that crushed all
our hopes that you would be
the next Gerber Baby

Things Your Parents Stole from the Hospital

WE TRIED TO TAKE THE NURSE HOME TOO

- [ ] 3,584 diapers (*you went through 293 in your first 24 hours*)

- [ ] Baby-swaddling blankets (*though not soft, they are strangely swaddle-able*)

- [ ] Nose-sucky thing (*it's more than a little alarming how many bodily fluids you produce and how long it will be until you can deal with them on your own*)

- [ ] Pacifiers/beanies/socks (*we raided the place*)

- [ ] Mesh underwear (*think breathable granny panties and horrible panty lines*)

- [ ] Three packages of the biggest sanitary napkins known to womankind

- [ ] Infectious-disease mouth masks (*no breathing on the baby!!*)

- [ ] Lady-parts numbing spray (*not sure why they didn't offer this during your delivery*)

- [ ] Spray water bottle for lady parts (*Mommy's life has taken a glamorous turn*)

- [ ] Other: _____

- [ ] Other: _____

Picture of You Heading Home

WE WERE A LITTLE ALARMED
THAT WE WERE ALLOWED TO TAKE YOU

*It's adorable how innocent
everyone still looks*

Our completely terrified thoughts as we took you home:

_____
_____
_____
_____
_____

How many miles under the speed limit we drove the whole way home: _____

Your First Visitors

YOU PEED ON ALL OF THEM

Visitor name: _____

Relationship to your parents:

☐ Family ☐ Friend ☐ Takeout delivery guy

What Visitor really thinks you look like:

_____

Visitor name: _____

Relationship to your parents:

☐ Family ☐ Friend ☐ FedEx driver

How many times your diaper or onesie had to be changed during the visit:

_____

Visitor name: _____

Relationship to your parents:

☐ Family ☐ Friend ☐ Girl Scout selling cookies

How quickly Visitor threw you back to Mommy when you started to cry:

_____

Visitor name: _____

Relationship to your parents:

☐ Family ☐ Friend ☐ Religious missionary

Ways Visitor thinks your parents are already messing you up:

_____

Visitor name: _____

Relationship to your parents:

☐ Family   ☐ Friend   ☐ Awkward coworker

How Visitor reacted when Mommy handed you over and took a nap:

_____

Visitor name: _____

Relationship to your parents:

☐ Family   ☐ Friend   ☐ Door-to-door sales rep

The piece of advice from Visitor that you probably shouldn't take:

_____

SOME VISIT HIGHLIGHTS

The first person whose spirit you broke with your incessant crying:

_____

How frightened your visitors were by the appearance of your parents:

_____

How disgusted your visitors were by the gory birth details shared:

_____

The first person you spit up on:

_____

The first person you peed on:

_____

The number of people who rethought their plans to have children as a direct result of you:

_____

Other: _____

This person had never held a baby before you (and will probably never hold one again)

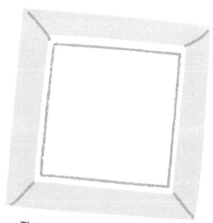

This person thought it might be dangerous to come into contact with the fluids you produced

You destroyed this person's shirt/pants/shoes/outfit (circle one) entirely

Other:
_____

Diary of Your First Week

IT WASN'T ALL ONESIES AND "WELCOME HOME" BALLOONS

DAY 1: We love you so much! Ways in which you are perfect:

_____

_____

DAY 2: Holy shit. How things got real today:

_____

_____

DAY 3: We're in over our heads. Ways in which we are failing:

_____

_____

DAY 4: Amount of sleep we've had since you arrived (*in minutes*):

_____

_____

DAY 5: All the things Mommy cried about today:

_____

_____

DAY 6: Mommy spent 6 days on the Web trying to understand these things about you: _____

_____

DAY 7: It's. Only. Been. Seven. Days. How many days (*in years*) it feels like:

_____

_____

LOOK WHAT YOU HAVE DONE

Your parents when they first met

DATE: ....

Your parents after one week with you

DATE: ....

Ways in Which You Are Not So Adorable

THE GERBER BABY YOU ARE NOT

- [ ] You never sleep
- [ ] You look nothing like an Anne Geddes photo
- [ ] You wait to pee or poop until *after* your diaper is removed
- [ ] You are horrible at holding up your end of the conversation
- [ ] All your smiles are gas-related
- [ ] Your screams have broken the eardrums of all the dogs in our zip code
- [ ] We've realized that the famous "new baby smell" is actually just a combination of sour milk, poop, and tears
- [ ] Other: _____
- [ ] Other: _____
- [ ] Other: _____

SLEEP DEPRIVED
THOUGHT OF THE DAY:

What are the odds Mommy has any idea what day it is today?

_____

PERSONAL BESTS

Your most annoying habit:

_____

The fastest you've ever ruined a onesie:

_____

Your shortest nap (*aka a blink*):

_____

The most times you made Mommy cry in one day:

_____

The longest amount of time you allowed us to put you down (*in seconds*):

_____

The most water you ever got on us during bath time:

_____

Adventures in Breastfeeding

YES, PEOPLE DO CRY OVER SPILLED MILK

The most inappropriate place you were breastfed:

_____

The furthest Mommy's boobs were sucked into her breast pump (*in feet*):

_____

The location of Mommy's boobs on her body before breastfeeding:

_____

The location of Mommy's boobs on her body after breastfeeding:

_____

The date you first bit Mommy's boob while breastfeeding:

_____

The most pumped breast milk ever accidentally spilled (*in gallons*):

_____

The date of Mommy's first nipple blister:

_____

Adventures in Bottle-Feeding

YOU HATED EVERY
"YOUR BABY WILL LOVE THIS" NIPPLE

The name of the first total stranger allowed to feed you while Mommy/Daddy did something else: _____

The first time we ran to the store while out and about because we forgot every damn bottle nipple at home (*date/how late this made us to where we were headed*): _____

The first time we forgot to screw the lid on the bottle and poured your meal on your face (*date/how many sound barriers your resulting scream broke*): _____

The first time we forgot to screw the lid on the bottle before shaking it and then splattered your meal all over the kitchen (*date/the symphony of curse words that this brought forth*): _____

The first time we found a very old half-full bottle somewhere in the house and considered calling a professional toxic-waste-removal team to dispose of it (*date/horrific smells coming from said bottle*): _____

Ways We Almost Killed You

IT'S A MIRACLE YOU SURVIVED US

Including, but not limited to, the following (*check all that apply*):

- [ ] Installed your car seat without assistance from the fire chief
- [ ] Lost control of your wobbly head and almost let it fall off
- [ ] Brought you home to the least-baby-proofed house ever
- [ ] Let you sleep too long/not long enough
- [ ] Co-slept
- [ ] Let you roll off Mommy's lap when she fell asleep breastfeeding you
- [ ] Let you roll off of the bed
- [ ] Tucked you in to the car seat but forgot to actually buckle you in
- [ ] Buckled you in to the car seat but forgot to actually buckle the seat to the car

SLEEP DEPRIVED
THOUGHT OF THE DAY:

What carefree activity were your parents doing a year ago today?

_____

- [ ] Was distracted and didn't notice your stroller roll into traffic
- [ ] Allowed the dog to lick inside your mouth
- [ ] Did not do enough tummy time (*you may never hold your head up*)
- [ ] Cut your fingernails too short (*extreme loss of blood*)
- [ ] Used 14 baby products that were later recalled
- [ ] Accidentally turned your swing on high and found out you're surprisingly aerodynamic
- [ ] Other: _____
- [ ] Other: _____

You and Forms of Media

BOOKS, SCREEN TIME, AND CUSS WORDS, OH MY!

NURTURING YOUR LITTLE BRAIN CELLS

The book you ate the most frequently:

_____

The book you destroyed like a savage animal:

_____

The book you wanted to hear on repeat that drove us insane:

_____

The book with the most ridiculous "plot":

_____

The 10-page book we can't believe we paid $20 for:

_____

The book that looked like it was illustrated by a drunk monkey:

_____

The first time we skipped more than half the pages of the book we were reading to you (*date/book*):

_____

DISTRACTING YOUR ENORMOUS SCREAM CELLS

The most annoying TV show theme song:

_____

The most annoying animated character:

_____

The most annoying live action character:

_____

The most ridiculous children's show concept:

_____

The most disturbing children's show concept:

_____

The children's show that is most obviously written by people under the influence of hallucinogens:

_____

How quickly you mastered selecting YouTube videos (_age in weeks_):

_____

How long (_in hours_) we stuck to our "No screen time for the baby" proclamation:

_____

Most inappropriate song we played to calm you down:

_____

Sleep

OR LACK THEREOF

The date we realized that sleeping 5–6 hours is considered "sleeping through the night" for a baby:

_____

How long we wept in each other's arms when we realized this (*in hours*):

_____

The longest one of us put off peeing because you'd fallen asleep on us and there was no way in hell we were going to risk waking you:

_____

The first time Mommy/Daddy army-crawled out of the room in an effort to not wake you (*date/injuries sustained because Mommy/Daddy have no upper body strength to speak of*):

_____

The first time we considered killing the UPS delivery person because they rang the doorbell while you were napping (*date/various cuss words hurled at said UPS delivery person*):

_____

The different sleep-training tactics we attempted before we gave up all hope of ever sleeping again (*check all that apply*):

☐ Baby-Wise Tactic (*scheduled feeding and eat/play/sleep*)
The amount of time (in minutes) it took you to make it known that you'd be in charge of all scheduling from here on out: _____

☐ Cry-It-Out Tactic (*pretty self-explanatory*)
The longest amount of time (in seconds) that Mommy/Daddy was actually able to let you cry before rushing to pick you up: _____

☐ The No-Cry Method (*aka The Hold-the-Baby-Until-It's-14-Years-Old Method*)
The record number of times Mommy/Daddy picked you up and put you down during one bedtime in an attempt to get you to sleep without crying: _____

☐ Other: _____
_____
_____
_____

Out and About

YOU TOOK THE WORLD BY STORM—AND SCREAM

The date we first tried to take you out of the house:

_____

How long it took us to pack the car:

_____

The date we first forgot to load you into the car before leaving the house:

_____

The date of your first public meltdown:

_____

The date we first took you to a restaurant:

_____

How quickly we had to leave said restaurant because of your behavior:

_____

How old you were when we officially decided that the only restaurant we were willing to go to was a drive-through:

_____

Longest amount of time you cried/shrieked in the back of a moving car where we couldn't reach or console you:

_____

Travel Attempts

THE HERMIT LIFE BECAME VERY APPEALING

The date of our first attempt at a road trip after you were born:

_____

How long (*in minutes*) we drove before we had to pull over to tend to your needs:

_____

How many stops you required throughout the road trip:

_____

The name of the city where we left a dirty diaper in a public place because there were no trash cans and we sure weren't taking it with us:

_____

Your first time in a hotel (*date/ways in which you made it clear you weren't a fan of overnight traveling*):

_____

The number of other hotel patrons who complained to the front desk about your screaming (*according to the desk clerk who called to ask if everything was okay—it was not*):

_____

Your first time on a plane (*date/why this was a horrible idea*):

_____

The cocktails we bought fellow passengers as an apology for your behavior:

_____

The first major family event we missed because traveling with you wasn't worth it:

_____

SO MUCH WORK FOR THINGS
THAT WILL FALL OUT

The date of the appearance of your first tooth:

_____

How many days you were possessed by the devil before said appearance
of first tooth:

_____

How many times a day one of us says, "I think the baby is teething" as an
excuse for your being horrible:

_____

How much saliva (*in gallons*) you produced daily while teething:

_____

The first person you bit with your new teeth:

_____

Mommy Before & After

AN ALARMING TRANSFORMATION

	BEFORE YOU ARRIVED	AFTER YOU ARRIVED
SHOWERS	The longest Mommy went between showers:	The longest Mommy went between showers:
CLOTHES	The number of "going out" outfits Mommy had in her closet:	The longest (*in weeks*) Mommy wore the same outfit 24 hours a day:
APPEARANCE	How often Mommy went to the hairdresser:	How long it's been since Mommy wore makeup:
FAVORITE ENRICHING ACTIVITIES	(*i.e. Sports/hobbies/crafts*)	(*i.e. Peeing alone/bathing/sleeping for longer than 25 minutes at a time*)
ADVENTURES	Some foreign countries Mommy visited:	Some foreign objects Mommy pulled from your mouth:
FRIDAY NIGHT	Favorite bar:	Favorite burp cloth:
SUNDAY MORNING	Best restaurant for brunch:	How long it's been since Mommy actually knew what day it was:

BEFORE BABY

AFTER BABY

Ways You Have Ruined Mommy

AN ARTISTIC INTERPRETATION

1. Draw Mommy's memory exiting her head.

2. Draw the 3 inches of exposed roots Mommy has because she hasn't gone to the hairdresser in months.

3. Shade in Mommy's new dark circles under her eyes.

4. Age Mommy's face by 15 years.

5. Draw Mommy's boobs in their new location.

6. Draw Mommy holding something poop- or vomit-covered.

7. Add Mommy's stretch marks.

8. Pad Mommy's thighs.

9. Erase or cross out Mommy's cute skirt. Then add pureed-peas-stained yoga pants.

10. Add Mommy's new—and much more sensible—shoes.

Ways You Soiled Yourself and Everything Around You

YOU LEFT YOUR MARK ON THE WORLD

The date when Mommy first unknowingly went out of the house with your poop on her clothes: _____

The date when Mommy first knowingly went out of the house with your poop on her clothes (*also known as The Day Mommy Officially Let Herself Go*):

_____

The longest amount of time one of us spent wrestling you into a onesie, only to have you soil it 30 seconds later:

_____

The date when you first shat up every single changing pad cover in the house before 10:00 a.m.: _____

The dates of the first times you spit up:

- On a complete stranger: _____

- On your parent's head: _____

- Down your parent's shirt: _____

- On your parent's plate of food: _____

- In your parent's mouth: _____

- And then rolled around in it: _____

Progression of Poop Diagram

MAY THESE DATES LIVE IN INFAMY

Top of head: the date your poop first went this high (*after which you were dipped in bleach*):

Ear: the date your poop first went this high (*yes, you pooped in your own ear*):

Top of diaper: the date your poop first went this high (*we had no idea this was the least of your abilities*):

Middle of head: the date your poop first went this high (*we're pretty sure the diaper isn't doing anything at all*):

Shoulder: the date your poop first went this high (*also the day we forgot your baby wipes*):

PERSONAL BESTS:

Most poopy diapers in one day: _____

Most onesies soiled in one day: _____

INNOCENCE ISN'T NECESSARILY PRETTY

Your first surprisingly colored poop (*date/color*):

_____

Your first projectile poop (*date/room it destroyed*):

_____

First time you pooped, peed, and puked all at once (*date/how long your diaper had been off—in seconds*):

_____

Your first unwarranted trip to the ER (*date/incident that prompted the visit*):

_____

What you ate before our first call to Poison Control:

_____

Your first haircut by your parents (*date/unfortunate results*):

_____

Your first emergency trip to an actual hairdresser to fix your first haircut by your parents (*date/hairdresser who came to your rescue*):

_____

The first milestone you hit embarrassingly late (*date/milestone/yes that date is correct*):

_____

PHOTOS OF YOUR FIRSTS

The first onesie you soiled
beyond redemption

You hating the taste
of your first food

The worst baby haircut
of all time

Other:

• 55 •

Your Parents' Firsts

THE BEGINNING OF THE END

Mommy's first mental breakdown following your birth:

DATE: _____

The first time Mommy googled "NIGHT NURSE":

DATE: _____

The first time we considered divorce following your birth:

DATE: _____

The first time we smelled your butt:

DATE: _____

The first time we picked your nose:

DATE: _____

The first time we used our spit to clean you:

DATE: _____

The first time we pooped in front of you/while holding you:

DATE: _____

The first time we forgot you somewhere:

DATE: _____

LOCATION: _____

Your Parents' Lasts

WE USED TO BE RESPECTED ADULTS

The last time we had sex:

DATE: _____

The last time we showered two days in a row:

DATE: _____

The last time we peed alone:

DATE: _____

The last time we set an alarm to wake up in the morning:

DATE: _____

The last time we looked like respectable adults:

DATE: _____

The last time we carried on an uninterrupted phone conversation:

DATE: _____

The last time we had a meal in a restaurant that didn't result in PTSD:

DATE: _____

The last time we *didn't* burst into laughter when someone asked,
"You have any big plans for this weekend?"

DATE: _____

Adventures in Eating

SOMETIMES YOU EVEN GOT FOOD IN YOUR MOUTH

The first food you ate:

_____

How quickly you spit it out:

_____

The date your parents thought it would be entertaining to watch you eat a lemon (*FYI: it was entertaining*):

_____

The first meal when you got more food on your body than in your body:

_____

The first food you threw across the room:

_____

Your favorite food to smear on your head:

_____

The date Mommy first googled "FULL-BODY BIB":

_____

The average amount of food (*in pounds*) on the dog's head at the end of every meal:

_____

The Most Disgusting Things You Put in Your Mouth

YOUR MOTTO WAS, "WHEN IN DOUBT, LICK IT"

Check all that apply:

☐ Pet's toy: _____

☐ Pet's food: _____

☐ Excrement: _____

☐ Bodily fluid: _____

☐ Regurgitated food: _____

☐ Dirt clod: _____

☐ Dust bunny: _____

☐ Dirty sock/underwear: _____

☐ Still unidentified item (*what it looked like*): _____

The Wide World of the Web

MOMMY'S NEW HOBBY:
2:00 a.m. INTERNET SEARCHES

Mommy googled the following (*check all that apply*):

☐ "Will my baby ever sleep?"

☐ "Long-term effects of sleep deprivation"

☐ "Long-term effects of giving baby just a tiny bit of gin"

☐ "Can babies die from crying too much?"

☐ "Can parents die from ramming their own heads against a nursery wall?"

☐ "How much infant feces is too much infant feces in my mouth?"

☐ "Night nurses on call in my area"

☐ "Vasectomy doctors in my area"

☐ Other: _____

☐ Other: _____

SLEEP DEPRIVED
THOUGHT OF THE DAY:

The Internet is a fun place
(full of reliable, reassuring
medical information)

Mommy diagnosed you with the following illnesses because she googled "BABY RASH" at 2:00 a.m. (*check all that apply*):

- [ ] Pinworm
- [ ] Hand, foot, and mouth disease
- [ ] Roseola
- [ ] Cradle cap
- [ ] Hepatitis
- [ ] Thrush
- [ ] Measles
- [ ] Polio
- [ ] Juvenile rheumatoid arthritis
- [ ] Mumps
- [ ] West Nile virus
- [ ] Scarlet fever
- [ ] Ringworm
- [ ] Dengue fever
- [ ] Reflux
- [ ] Ear infection
- [ ] Pinkeye
- [ ] Jaundice
- [ ] Other: _____
- [ ] Other: _____

Ways You Demonstrated Absolutely No Regard for Your Own Well-Being

IT'S A MIRACLE YOU SURVIVED YOURSELF

You (*check all that apply*):

- ☐ Gouged your eyes with your fingernails
- ☐ Repeatedly tried to roll off any high location you could find
- ☐ Thought pulling a cat's tail was a good idea
- ☐ Never met an object you didn't immediately try to choke on
- ☐ Never met a diseased surface you didn't want to lick
- ☐ Weren't totally opposed to consuming your own feces
- ☐ Set a personal goal to escape your crib/high chair/moving swing
- ☐ Challenged gravity to a duel on the stairs
- ☐ Other: _____

Your Injuries

GRAVITY WAS NOT A FRIEND OF YOURS

The date of your first major head injury: _____

The longest stretch of time you went with a
unicorn-looking bump on your forehead:

_____

The date of your first black eye:

_____

The first time we googled "BABY HELMET":

_____

The date of your first bloody nose: _____

The date of your first fat lip: _____

The date when Mommy/Daddy first blurted out,
"I swear I don't beat my baby!" to a stranger
because you were covered in bruises:

_____

The date you first slammed your own
finger in a door: _____

The date we first called the advice
nurse about your injuries: _____

PERSONAL
BESTS:

The most bumps and
bruises you had
at one time: _____

The most Band-Aids
you required in
one day: _____

Your First Holidays

AREN'T TRADITIONS ADORABLE?

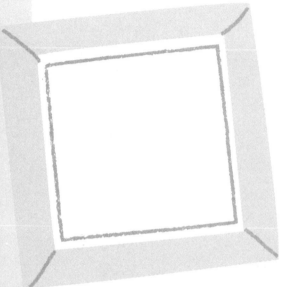

You horrified with Santa

You horrified with the Easter Bunny

You traumatized by fireworks

You crying in your first Halloween costume

Your Ridiculous First Birthday Party

A RITUAL IN WHICH A CONFUSED BABY IS FORCED TO SMEAR CAKE EVERYWHERE

The elaborate theme of your first birthday party: _____

How many people attended your first birthday party: _____

How many times you did the following at your big party:

- Cried: _____

- Napped: _____

- Pooped your pants: _____

- Ripped off your annoying "First Birthday" gear: _____

- Screamed in terror when handed to a partygoer: _____

- Expressed complete disinterest in one of your adorable presents: _____

I SURVIVED *my parents'* 1st YEAR!

How horrified you were when everyone started singing "Happy Birthday" to you:

[1] ···· [2] ···· [3] ···· [4] ···· [5] ···· [6] ···· [7] ···· [8] ···· [9] ···· [10]

MILDLY CONFUSED

FOR THE REST OF YOUR LIFE YOU WILL
HAVE NIGHTMARES ABOUT A LARGE
CHANTING GROUP OF GIANTS COMING
AT YOU WITH A PLATE OF FIRE

How willing you were to shove cake in your face:

[1] ···· [2] ···· [3] ···· [4] ···· [5] ···· [6] ···· [7] ···· [8] ···· [9] ···· [10]

YOU HUMORED THE CHANTING
GIANTS BY PUTTING A LITTLE
FROSTING ON YOUR NOSE

YOU SENT A STRONG MESSAGE
TO THE CHANTING GIANTS BY
DISMEMBERING SAID CAKE IN A
RATHER HORRIFYING FASHION

Our family on your first birthday

Our family on your first day

Journal of Your First Year

IT WAS THE BEST OF TIMES, IT WAS THE LONGEST OF YEARS. EVER.

MONTH 1

Highlights: _____

_____

_____

_____

_____

_____

_____

_____

Lowlights: _____

_____

_____

_____

_____

_____

_____

MONTH 2

Highlights: _____

_____

_____

_____

_____

_____

_____

_____

_____

_____

_____

Lowlights: _____

_____

_____

_____

_____

_____

_____

_____

_____

_____

MONTH 3

Highlights: _____

_____

_____

_____

_____

_____

_____

_____

_____

_____

Lowlights: _____

_____

_____

_____

_____

_____

_____

_____

_____

_____

MONTH 4

Highlights: _____
_____
_____
_____
_____
_____
_____
_____
_____
_____

Lowlights: _____
_____
_____
_____
_____
_____
_____
_____
_____

MONTH 5

Highlights: _____

_____

_____

_____

_____

_____

_____

_____

_____

_____

Lowlights: _____

_____

_____

_____

_____

_____

_____

_____

_____

_____

MONTH 6

Highlights: _____

_____

_____

_____

_____

_____

_____

_____

_____

Lowlights: _____

_____

_____

_____

_____

_____

_____

_____

_____

MONTH 7

Highlights: _____

_____

_____

_____

_____

_____

_____

_____

_____

_____

_____

Lowlights: _____

_____

_____

_____

_____

_____

_____

_____

_____

_____

MONTH 8

Highlights: _____

_____

_____

_____

_____

_____

_____

_____

_____

_____

Lowlights: _____

_____

_____

_____

_____

_____

_____

_____

_____

_____

MONTH 9

Highlights: _____

_____

_____

_____

_____

_____

_____

_____

_____

_____

_____

Lowlights: _____

_____

_____

_____

_____

_____

_____

_____

_____

_____

_____

MONTH 10

Highlights: _____

_____

_____

_____

_____

_____

_____

_____

_____

_____

Lowlights: _____

_____

_____

_____

_____

_____

_____

_____

_____

MONTH 11

Highlights: _____

_____

_____

_____

_____

_____

_____

_____

_____

_____

Lowlights: _____

_____

_____

_____

_____

_____

_____

_____

_____

_____

MONTH 12

Highlights: _____

_____

_____

_____

_____

_____

_____

_____

_____

_____

_____

_____

Lowlights: _____

_____

_____

_____

_____

_____

_____

_____

_____

_____

_____

YOUR FAMILY TREE

1 _____
2 _____
3 _____
4 _____
5 _____
6 _____
7 _____
8 _____
(No one knows how this person is related to us, but they always show up to family events.)